Before You Take The Plunge

What your minister, counselor, teachers, family, friends and society should have told you about marriage and relationships – but didn't.

By Stephen M. Dupree

Copyright © 2011 by Stephen M. Dupree

Cover design by S.M. Dupree & Sheila Lutringer
Book design by S.M. Dupree & Sheila Lutringer
Cover photo by Gary Heatherly

All rights reserved.

No part of this publication may be reproduced, distributed, or transmitted in any form or by any means, including photocopying, recording, or other electronic or mechanical methods, without the prior written permission of the author or publisher, except in the case of brief quotations embodied in critical reviews and certain other noncommercial uses permitted by copyright law. For permission requests, write to the author, addressed, Attention: Permissions Coordinator, at the web address below.

No animals, insects, humans or plants were intentionally harmed in creating this work however, trillions of electrons were horribly inconvenienced.

S.M. Dupree
Visit my website at www.smdupree.com &
www.beforeyoutaketheplunge.com

Printed in the United States of America

First Printing: June 2011
Stony River Media
Asheville, North Carolina
StonyRiverMedia.com

Dupree, Stephen M.
Before You Take The Plunge : What your minister, counselor, teachers, family, friends and society should have told you about marriage and relationships - but didn't. S.M. Dupree.

ISBN: 978-0-9844968-1-5

Acknowledgements

I gave serious consideration to just not doing this page. Then I thought perhaps that I could get away with a general, blanket thank you. I was prevailed upon though, to at least make the effort to acknowledge those with a critical role in bringing this project together. There are a lot and there was no way that I would be successful in including all the names of those deserving of mention. It has been a long time since I could validly claim to have done anything on my own except make mistakes. My successes, such as they are, are built upon the support of others, some here and now, others that preceded me. For this project my siblings, my friends who read excerpts and encouraged me, my friends who kept me fed and taken care of after my accident, and of course all those who have entrusted me with a major role in a critical part of their lives plus many more are deserving of individual mention. That sentence alone though, describes way more names than you would read if, against all odds, I was able to list them all. It does not describe all of those whose efforts and/or tolerance got me to the starting line.

My sister Claretta Y. Dupree, friends Noel Hudson and Laura Still agreed to be my editors for this project even though they all know me. Sheila Lutringer took pity on my aesthetics challenged skill set and agreed to do the layout and design of the book. Troy & Jackie were the couple who beat me up into agreeing to perform their nuptials and Dave & Jessamy were the actual first couple whose ceremony I officiated. Brian Conley gave me my first writing gig in his (at the time) alt weekly, *Metropulse*. My friend Robert Loest challenged me and encouraged me and gifted me with the laptop computer on which I wrote the lion's share of this book. This book is dedicated to his memory.

Table of Contents

Introduction 8
Why Marry? 14
The Difference Between Marriage and Wedding 19
Trust & Communications 23
Breaking The Language Barrier 32
Desire & Expectation 39
Commonalities & Differences 44
Money 53
Pets & Children 61
Courtesy 65
Continuation of Dating 70
An Approach to Serious Communications 76
Closing Thoughts 79
Appendix 83

Foreword

On the bank of the Kentucky River, with my lovely bride standing between me and the author of this book, on a fine summer day with family and friends gathered around, a wedding was held to celebrate our marriage. If referring to a wedding celebrating a marriage sits awkwardly on your mind then you should definitely read this book.

My journey to that day of celebration includes nearly thirty years ministering in a mainstream Protestant denomination, which shall remain nameless out of respect for the possibility that they are not as proud of my years of service as I am. The only reason I bring it up is to say that over those three decades I saw and or participated in a lot of marriage ceremonies and witnessed the good, bad, and outright ugly of premarital and relationship counseling. So it is with some authority that I can say the content of this book is some of the best I have ever encountered. But that isn't why I would recommend this book to anyone even remotely interested in its topic. To recommend it on that basis would be to focus its relevance on institutional dogma and subject it to the biases peculiar to religious institutions. Both the author and the book deserve better than that. That being said, it isn't that the content is contrary to most religious beliefs, rather it is the context. Living out the principles set forth in this book will not hinder you on whatever spiritual path you have chosen but neither have they been set forth to make you right with the great creator. Herein lies a truth designed to make you right with yourself.

I first became acquainted with the concepts presented here in a local brewpub while consuming some of the finest Porter I have ever had. I listened to the reasoned and sometimes impassioned discourse of the author as he also consumed a pint or two. Do not be mislead, however, and think that the ideas, notions, and philosophies in this book are the product of alcohol induced ravings. Rather, they are the byproduct of a genuine concern that far too many people are unprepared for the hard work involved in having a truly meaningful relationship, filled with mutual respect and adoration that can last through the obstacle course of life. I only mentioned the Porter because I ended up trading one of my beloved mugs from my Mug Club membership as payment for services in my own marriage ceremony.

I entertain the notion that many years from now I will approach death and my bride will be able to lovingly hold my hand and ease my journey into another existence; and that even after years of living with me I will actually deserve her love and respect. If that be the case I am convinced that it will at least be due in part to my meeting Steve Dupree and engaging him in one of his favorite pastimes; waxing eloquent on all things logical, especially those contained in this book. That being said, I fully comprehend that if I am able to realize my wish of mutually shared enduring marital bliss it will not be because I read this book or knew the author. It will be because the principles are sound and, more importantly, I believed them to be so. Read this book with the knowledge that in this case knowing is not enough. It will be in the acting on these guidelines that you will find a measure of success. How much and how soon will be up to you.

John Goins

Introduction

A number of years ago I was working in a small office with a couple of other guys and the boss. One day while the boss was out, the three of us worker bees all went to the Universal Life Church website (www.ulc.org) and signed up to become ordained ministers. We each printed out our certificates of ordination and yukked it up a bit. (The boss was informed immediately upon his return and recruited to join us but he firmly declined.) Later on after work, either that day or subsequent days, I showed off my certificate to friends at the local watering hole. At some point, some friends who were engaged to be married asked me if I would officiate at their nuptials since I was an ordained minister. I declined saying that I didn't really take it seriously. My oldest sister actually ended up officiating at that wedding.

That was just the beginning of requests that I perform that duty. Several friends asked and each time I declined. Some argued that I was a great choice for the job even given my stated attitude towards my ordination but still I declined. Some of my friends however were more tenacious than others. They continued to ask over a long engagement that I officiate at their ceremony. Other friends that we had in common chimed in in support of the idea of me officiating. The pressure mounted until it was all but continuous. Under the influence of such pressure from friends, and a few beers, I capitulated. I agreed to perform their ceremony. As soon as some other friends who were not in that particular group heard, they insisted that since I was going to do that ceremony, I could do theirs as well and it was off to the races.

The second couple's wedding date was actually before the first couple's, so they became the first of my (estimated) some thirty odd weddings to date. The nature of who I am does not allow me to consider half measures so I searched the Internet for wedding vows and readings. I read through several ceremonies to get a feel for what went where. I presented several options to the couples and talked to them about what they wanted in their ceremony. I even composed some thoughts of my own and inserted them as appropriate (by my estimation) in the ceremonies. Most of my subsequent requests to officiate came from those who were in attendance at weddings I officiated so I have to assume that I was doing a good job.

Three or four weddings in, it was made known to me that marriage licenses in my state were available at a significant discount if the couple had premarital counseling. Naturally, I thought, "I can do that." I could offer the counseling and either pocket the money they saved or just reduce their overall cost, whichever seemed most appropriate (from each according to their ability ...). A rational person would probably have just signed off on the counseling and assumed that the couples were adult enough to know what they wanted and work out their issues. However, as I mentioned before, it just ain't in me to do half measures. I starting thinking about what things couples really ought to think about prior to getting married, especially those things that were unlikely to have been mentioned by someone else. I made a few notes but generally they were simply one or two word reminders of issues I wanted to address. The actual counseling was pretty free form.

Though I was counseling folks up to my own age and folks who had previous marriages under their belts, I pretty consistently heard that what I was telling them was either brand new stuff or at least presented in a way that they had not considered. I was even referred to do the counseling of a couple whose nuptials I was not officiating. The more I did it, the more I thought I should have some sort of consistency and make sure that I hit all of the salient points each time. Obviously, that was going to require some organization. It was also going to require a system that did not depend on my (notoriously bad) moment-to-moment memory. I was going to have to work from actual comprehensive clear notes. Of course, it would really be nice to have something to hand to the couples that they could refer back to later and not have to depend on their note taking skills and/or memory (although I certainly told all of them they could contact me for a refresher whenever they wanted/needed).

Upon thinking about the idea of clear and comprehensive printed materials, the thought of a book came unbidden to my mind. To be fair, I have a bunch of books, physical and electronic, so the idea of a book is never really that far from my mind; it is just that usually I'm thinking of reading one. Unlike untold numbers of my ideas, I actually acted on this one, albeit months and months after the initial idea.

That is essentially how I now find myself in the situation of offering advice on how to successfully conduct a marriage to those about to marry though at this point, I have never actually been in a marriage. I feel it is only fair to point out that the overwhelming majority of Catholic priests who offer similar services have also never been married and most of them have even less experience of intimate dealings with the opposite sex than I do. But most of what I offer here is not actually specific to marriage. I think that most of it can be applied, either as is or with a little modification, to any of a variety of relationships. I believe if one is to find truth, one must be open to it. Placing constraints as to where the truth may originate is counter-productive to the goal of finding it.

So, why will this book help? Good question. Much of what is considered counseling, for relationships and other issues, involves telling you how to address problems that have come up or that will probably come up. The approach in this book is different. What I suggest, if fully implemented, should prevent a lot of the problems common to relationships from ever coming up. This approach is different because the "traditional" approach has us nationally at an approximate divorce rate of 50%.

The answer to the "why" then is a little complex but is basically, it works. The suggestions presented here are not incompatible with any approach that recognizes the equality of the individuals. I do not suggest or require that anyone renounce or take up religious or political beliefs. There is an old line about the difficulty of being up to your rear end in alligators and remembering that your original objective was to drain the swamp. Once you are already in a relationship, you may not have the time or focus to figure these things out on your own. I do not propose controversial or drastic changes in actions and attitudes. If you have gotten far enough in your relationship to be considering long term planning, drastic changes are not indicated. My suggestions will give you the framework that allows you to get maximum enjoyment and minimum stress from your relationship(s).

I think it will be difficult to be 100% true to the concepts I present here but certainly not impossible. Though I have written them, at times I found myself asking why no one had told me those things instead of just letting me screw up a succession of relationships of a certain type. However, if a couple will read this and think about what I put forth here, I believe that it will lead them to an understanding and tolerance for each other that significantly enhances their chance for a successful and long lasting relationship.

Choose love, choose happiness, choose peace.

Why Marry?

I have spent much of my life wondering why people get married. When I started writing the wedding ceremonies of friends and officiating at those weddings, the question(s) remained unanswered to my satisfaction. Individuals, when asked why they wanted to get married, would reply with an answer that was highly specific to them (and sometimes incoherent) which was exactly what I wasn't looking for. I wanted a blanket answer, something that could apply to most anyone seeking to formalize a relationship. Rather obviously, my approval or understanding of why someone wants to marry was not and is not required. My thinking however, was that if I was going to officiate, or even just attend and help my friends celebrate, it would be better if I was able to buy in completely and for that, I needed understanding.

I understand being in love. I have been crazy in love but, even in the depths of my amorous insanity, I understood that to marry simply as a way to trap the object of my affection was not a high enough purpose. I understood that I was uninterested in constructing an emotional prison where I could incarcerate that special someone. Perhaps I am a bit insecure but I have always wanted, have always needed to know that the woman with me was there only because that is exactly where she wanted to be. I needed to know that in full and active awareness of all of her options, she chose to be with me. I needed to know that I was not making a decision of whom to be with out of laziness, of doing what was easy. I had to know that I was not with her because I was afraid of being alone or that I was leery of the potential work and trauma involved in a breakup.

So what I needed in response to my question was an answer that would work for me. Why would someone like me choose to formalize a relationship with a young lady though that relationship, prior to the formalization, was not obviously lacking anything? There are the obvious legal ramifications but anyone can hire a lawyer to draw up contracts of cooperation and joint ownership and such. I have heard people called "bastard", but only as an intentional insult of varying intensity. I have never been asked as a part of a job interview whether or not my parents were wed at the time of my conception or birth, nor when I have been the interviewer, did I make that inquiry of job applicants. I have never based a ballot box decision on the marital status of the candidate's parents at the time of his or her birth. I have been able to share a hotel room without proving marriage. On top of everything else, in many places in this nation, if you live together long enough, you become "common law" spouses. You are for all intent and purposes married. So why formalize the relationship with a wedding or a legalized commitment?

Eventually, I had to develop my own reasoning, my own understanding of why I would consider such a thing (although at the time of this writing, I have not yet formalized any of the relationships I have had). I believe that the act of marrying someone is the equivalent of taking a handshake agreement and turning it into a full fledged business agreement with a contract. Think of a couple of guys working on an idea in a garage. Initially, there is enough excitement about the idea to sustain the energy that the work requires. Eventually though, especially as the idea nears fruition, the question of who has put in how much comes around. One guy owns the garage and has been paying the utilities. The other may have actually had the original idea. Each of them may have a skill set that the other doesn't, perhaps one is the designer and the other is a fabricator. One skill may require more mental effort and the other more physical. As they get closer to having a viable product and company, they have to start thinking about the compensation structure and how to make that fair given their respective levels of effort and contribution. They may well resort to a contract that seeks to "normalize" what they have done so far so that moving forward, they are on exactly equal footing.

That normalization is my understanding of why to marry. In a relationship, one person is the first to say "I love you". One person is typically more demonstrative than the other. In any relationship, each individual brings different "stuff" to the relationship. The act of getting married brings the participants to equal footing. They can each reference a specific level of commitment that the other brings to the relationship. They are each willing to publicly proclaim their devotion to the other regardless of what their friends or families think of the choices they have made.

An awful lot of what one gets in a marriage is available with no contract or ceremony, as is the marriage. Cohabitation, kids, respect of friends and/or family, the general sharing of resources, all of that and more can happen without the traditional ceremony, but it can also happen while one or both partners have questions about the level of commitment of the other. The wedding doesn't actually change anything but your understanding. Once it takes place, you can say that the Other is at least a known level of commitment. Your partner may be more committed than that, as may you, but you know the two of you are at least that committed and you and your relationship can grow from there.

The Difference Between Wedding and Marriage

It seems a simple thing and an obvious thing but, there seems to be some confusion about a wedding and a marriage. I hear the words used incorrectly (to some degree) fairly frequently. Clarity of the concepts can only enhance the probability of the success of the relationship.

The Marriage

A marriage is the outward expression over time of the commitment made in the context of a relationship. The marriage is a formalized relationship. The formalization of the relationship can take place in any two of three places (or all three). In this culture, the legal aspects of marriage loom large. It provides for certain remedies under the law for any of several potential problems from outside the relationship such as powers of attorney, hospital visitation, and general financial issues. Should one participant in the relationship fail to act in good faith, or if the relationship should fail for whatever reason, the legalities serve as a buffer against some of the harsher realities of the world for the weaker partner. Obviously, the legal arena is one place and in theory, issues there are simplified by the formalization.

The relationship can be formalized in the religious sense. It can represent the endorsement of a given church or denomination on a couple's commitment. The importance of such a thing to individuals or families who value that is incalculable. The recognition of the church can put an individual (or couple) in a frame of mind that makes them more amenable to putting serious effort into maintaining the communication and trust necessary for making a sustained relationship work.

The third place for the formalization to take place is the most important. It is within the individual. Only a fool would marry someone that was not committed to him or to whom he is not committed. A common misconception is that the commitment happens at the wedding. If it does, I predict the early failure of the relationship. If you conceptualize the night prior to your wedding as your last night of freedom, you aren't ready for marriage. Once you have internally made the decision to be committed, you are ready. It does not, DOES NOT work to decide to be committed next week. You are either deciding to be committed now or you are deciding to not be committed now.

When one is in a truly mutually committed

relationship, one is finally free to love as one deems appropriate. You are no longer constrained by the fears and insecurities that fuel so many stories of teen-aged and early adult angst. While the responsibilities that begin or expand immediately following the wedding should certainly be soberly considered and understood, if you are afraid of them or if you dread the onset of those responsibilities, you may not yet be ready for marriage. When the liberation that a properly understood marriage confers is foremost in your mind, when that is more important to you than any trepidation you might feel about the added responsibilities, then marriage may reasonably be considered.

The Wedding
A wedding is a ceremony. It is a ceremony celebrating and acknowledging the commitment that the couple has already made. Historically, it has been one of the markers of transition into full adulthood. Weddings have been used to celebrate the peace or other agreement between tribes. A wedding does not make a marriage any more than giving someone a medal makes them a hero. The wedding follows the marriage. Though traditionalists might prefer that the sexual consummation of the commitment not happen until

after the wedding, the commitment has to happen first. Without the commitment, there is nothing to celebrate, no reason to lay out a huge expenditure of money and effort and time to create the party, no reason to plan a special church service to thank God for the union of the couple. While the wedding may be important to some of the friends and family, it in no way makes the marriage. It is frequently an added stress to the still evolving relationship and can actually do more harm than good. Still, for those who value such a thing, the wedding ceremony can be a time of reflection and a time for family and friends to commit their support to the couple who have committed to each other.

The difference between a marriage and a wedding is the same as the difference between an education and a diploma. Without the diploma, you still know just as much but the public may not acknowledge or respect your knowledge. For some that public acknowledgement has little value and for others it is important. The thing to take away is that a diploma with no education behind it is merely worthless paper. A marriage certificate with no commitment behind it is a scam. It would be far better to have a big expensive party where everyone knew that no marriage would take place than to fake a marriage with or without the wedding.

Trust and Communication

There are only two components to every relationship. Every relationship, every human interpersonal relationship, can be defined in terms of type and levels of these two things. As there are only these two things, every relationship MUST have both.

Let's say you're walking down the street. You are in your neighborhood. You see someone approaching that does not look familiar to you. It isn't one of your neighbors and to the best of your knowledge, you have never communicated with him. You have no relationship with this person. You pass without incident. On subsequent days, on subsequent walks, you repeatedly see the same person. At some point, you start to nod at him in passing confirming that you have established visual communication. Once you have passed several times without incident, you get to the point of expecting or trusting there to be no incidents. At this stage, you have a relationship. It is a very basic relationship. It may be all that it ever will or it may simply be the foundation upon which a more complex and involved relationship will be built, but what is important is that you now have a relationship. You have trust and you have communication. Those are the two things that you must have if a relationship is to take place.

Communication Basics

There are of course, many types and levels of communication. The visual communication in the example above could be be expanded so that details of mannerisms and gait and style of dress are noted which would represent a different level of visual communication. If you get to the point of waving at the individual, that adds another little point to the visual communication and of course, when the actions and acknowledgements are reciprocated, it is more definitive.

Speech is a pretty obvious communication type. It might start with a simple "morning" in passing and escalate to polite conversations about the weather or neighborhood concerns. From there as the relationship grows, conversations about local sports, politics, arts, your professions and families may ensue. Eventually, if the relationship reaches that point, there may be verbal expressions of affection and dedication. Verbal communication is how most of us will communicate on a day to day basis in all of our close relationships. I am going to cheat a bit and include the written word in this category even though it could stand on its own. Texting, talking, emailing, video conferencing, and other forms of messaging are at our finger and tongue tips and may all be reasonably considered to be speech. Oddly enough, with all the speech communications options open to us, we still foolishly use the phrase "Well it goes without saying that ...". If one thinks or actually speaks that phrase, it is a clear indication that it should NOT go without saying. Things which are not explicitly stated should not be assumed to be understood. It is fine to hope for them to be understood. You may think your audience probably understands. However, things that are important, things that underpin your expectations, should not be left to chance. There may be those who are so close that they actually seem to read each other's minds, but I have not observed any of them. I have seen couples that appeared very close, displaying affection and respect for each other, couples in a long-term relationship, and one partner will completely misunderstand what the other wanted or expected of them. When it is important, be explicit.

Touch is a form of communication. The handshake you might offer early on is said to have began as a way of notifying someone you encountered in passing that you were not bearing weapons. The pat on the back is recognized in our culture as communicating appreciation of a job well done. A hug might communicate sympathy, joy, growing affection or appreciation. If the touching continues and escalates in intimacy from handshakes to hugs to kisses to massage and more, eventually you reach the pinnacle of the "touch" pyramid, the act of sexual intercourse or making love. In combination with strong emotion and perhaps other forms of communication, it can be the ultimate communication of togetherness and commitment.

Our propensity for associating relatively unrelated things because of their chronological concurrence makes smell and taste potentially important means of communication. The perfume of a loved one can bring back vivid and explicit memories and emotions even when experienced in ways unrelated to said loved one. The same might be said of a particular meal or treat, even the taste of your lover's mouth when you kiss or the smell of his or her hair.

All of it is communication and all of it can bolster or reinforce the other forms of communication. Of course, they can also be the source of confusion in the case of perceived "mixed signals." For these reasons, attention should be paid to what you are communicating as well as to the intent of the other person and what they are attempting to communicate.

Trust Basics

In our example of the person you pass on the street, you start with no trust. NOT mistrust, because mistrust, like trust, must be earned. You neither trust nor mistrust. As your encounters on the street continue and nothing bad or out of the ordinary happens, you begin to trust, or expect, that encounters with the individual will be ordinary. Once you are to the point of exchanging pleasantries, you begin to trust that your encounters will be pleasant. As your verbal communication grows in amount and complexity, you may well trust your encounters to be intellectually challenging or emotionally uplifting or spiritually edifying. As your trust grows, you become more comfortable with the idea of different kinds of communication. Sooner or later, you may trust the individual enough to allow a touch, from a handshake to a pat on the back, a brief hug to a sustained hug, even to a kiss. All of that represents a growing level of trust and serves to enable different kinds and intensities of communication, all the way to the act of making love which, whether it is intended or not, is an expression of ultimate trust.

Trust AND Communication

In the formative relationship, these two things, trust and communication, are synergistic. Each will build on the other and if one stagnates or regresses, it will likely have that same effect on the other. You tend to not talk much to those whom you do not trust and you certainly do not want them touching you. On the other hand, it is the nature of relationships to grow and change and there is every chance that you will not trust a person with whom your level and type of communication is always the same.

While all of that is interesting, that is not what is important. What is important is the idea that while there are many types of communication, trust is just trust. Like any of several types of communication, it has a whole range of intensity but, unlike communication, there is only one type. What is important is the knowledge that a relationship MUST consist of both of those things. If you do not have both, you do not have a relationship. If you lose one of those things, you do not have a relationship.

You could feasibly lose the ability to speak or hear and still have a very meaningful relationship. There are examples in recent memory of one of a couple losing the ability to move yet maintaining a meaningful relationship. Many couples stay together long after they no longer engage in sexual intercourse. One type of communication can substitute for another completely or in part. However, NO relationship can survive a lack of trust! If in fact you lose trust, you simply do not have a relationship and no amount of lying to yourself or others will make it so. The same would be true if you lost all communication but that typically requires the intent of one or more participants of the relationship. The loss of trust, regardless of the intent of the precipitating event, is the end of the relationship. It may be possible to build another relationship, but that one is gone and gone forever.

For this reason, I cannot possibly state strongly enough that each participant in a relationship must jealously, attentively and intentionally GUARD YOUR TRUST. You can neither casually mistrust your partner nor negligently give your partner reason to mistrust. Either one WILL kill the relationship. Trust is irreplaceable. Until you are willing to take trust seriously, from both sides, you are not ready for a relationship and the guaranteed result is pain - deep, abiding, and quite likely to be unforgiven pain. If that is not your goal, you must constantly consider trust.

Was It All A Big Mistake?

The universe is a multi-dimensional place. If you go from one location to another location, though you may not be actively aware of it, physical distance is not the only thing that passes. Everything around you changes with the passage of time and/or with use, wear and tear if you will. For this reason, there really is no going back. There are no "do overs." If you go from one place to another place, physically, emotionally, intellectually or otherwise, and you decide that you do not like the second place, you must start where you are and move to where (you think) you want to be. If you used to have a relationship with a person and one of you destroyed the trust (or completely ceased communications), and a relationship with each other is something the two of you still desire, you must start from where you are and go to where you want to be. You will have to date. You will have to rediscover that which you have in common and in difference. You will have to honestly discuss all of those things that any couple in the formative stages of a relationship would discuss. Nothing should be taken for granted or assumed simply because of your prior relationship. Beginning a relationship with the memory of a breech of trust still fresh is a difficult thing to do but that difficulty is just one of the reasons you must take the trust in your relationship so seriously. It is why you must constantly consider it. The bloom of love obscures for many the sacrifices made and the compromises readily agreed to, but if you find yourself in the situation of building anew a relationship that an abuse of trust has destroyed, all of that will be starkly revealed. A relationship in which trust has been lost will never again be as it was the first time. The intensity is possibly gone, the naiveté definitely so. Efforts taken within a relationship to avoid the necessity of doing the job without the natural numbing agents make nothing but good sense.

Again, I cannot stress strongly enough, the protective attitude you need to have toward the trust in your relationships. Gold, diamonds or a Ferrari's paint job are less painful to lose and easier to restore. Guard your trust or lose your relationship. Period.

Breaking The Language Barrier

Over the years in several situations I have been exposed to a variety of languages. In high school Spanish classes early on an effort was made to teach us to trill when we had to make the "r" sound. It was not a skill that came easily to everyone but it was nowhere near as difficult as a lot of the foreign sounds I was to encounter later on. Some cultures have a downright creative approach to the use of consonants. Others appear to have their pay based on the number of vowel sounds they emit every time their mouths open.

The strangeness of a language was something that you just had to get past. Sometimes learning or at least familiarizing yourself with a language was part of the job. Sometimes it was what you had to do to comfortably live where you happened to be. Either way you did what was necessary although in my case, it was usually no more than necessary. To that end, a lot of the time I learned to understand much more of the local language than I could actually speak.

This is a lesson that would be well learned in relationships. The truth is, not everyone speaks the same language in relationships. There are gross generalizations that can be made and will probably be accurate more often than not. Men are generally not as verbally expressive as women. Women are usually thought to be less physically expressive than men. I could go on about the general approach any of several subcultures take to relationships. As I have noted in other places, the mere fact that these things may be differences does not mean that they must serve as permanent separators.

A common thing about relationships, especially relationships that may lead to marriage, is that differences abound between the principals. Even those you might think appear to have everything in common will have humongous differences. Dog or cat, sweet or savory, spicy or mild, action or romance, rock or blues, BMW or Mercedes, Merlot or Riesling, Windows or Mac, all of these things and a thousand more could be differences in a couple that most anyone would describe as having much in common. The differences are as likely to make the Other interesting to us as they are to be a source of irritation. If you can learn to accept and understand those differences, not try to change or eliminate them so that you don't have any differences but accept and understand that you are different, then things can start to get serious.

BREAKING THE LANGUAGE BARRIER

I have known couples who have been together a long time that seem to have survived by staking out a territory and spending their "spare" time there. Frequently the garage or workshop is the domain of the male and the kitchen or sewing or craft room is the domain of the female. He might restore cars or motorcycles or build furniture. She might learn gourmet cooking or make all the dresses for her relatives weddings. Obviously that is no where near a comprehensive list of the potential activities but it will do as an example. What that couple is doing, whether they realize it or not, is speaking different languages. Their lives will be enhanced if they learn to accept and understand the Other's language even if as I noted above, they cannot speak it. Consider this: a man gets up on a Saturday morning and pulls his Other's car into their garage. He proceeds to change the oil, rotate the tires, and wash the car. What would a proper response be? I maintain that it would be well and proper for the female to say, "I love you too, honey." If it happened that way, it would mean that she had accepted and learned to understand his language. Of course, it would also work if she had worked in the hot kitchen for hours to prepare his favorite meal. As a matter of fact, she might do that in return for the automotive maintenance. Those actions, the speaking of one's natural language, might reasonably be considered the relationship equivalent of an "in kind" contribution. As such, they are not inherently worth more, or less, than the expression in an Other's language. He expresses his love using his language and she expresses her love using hers. As long as they both understand, it's a beautiful thing.

We spend far too much time and effort trying to force others to speak our language. It is bad enough when it is literally a spoken language and we are trying to homogenize it to a common level of incorrectness. But when we are dealing with the language of relationships, it is downright disgusting and seriously detrimental. Something in the cultural minutia of this nation makes it difficult for a lot of men to speak the words "I love you." It does not, to the best of my knowledge, make those men any less likely to love. It does not appear to make them any less likely to express that love in other ways. If you focus on the spoken words and in effect claim that only they matter, eventually you will probably be correct. Your refusal to learn the language your Other is using and his strong reluctance to the words you insist must be used will unfortunately lead to the realization that you are not communicating. Since you must have trust and communication to have a relationship it would mean that your relationship is done. I do not mean to suggest that men are without responsibility in issues of this nature. We must also make the effort to accept and understand that the way we speak to our buddies with a wrench in hand or as we toss a football back and forth is likely to not be effective in communicating to our Other. If you know that phrase spoken aloud is hugely important to your Other, then even if you are uncomfortable saying it, sometimes you will just have to suck it up and deal with the discomfort. It simply is not a situation where it is all one way or the other. Both parties (or in the case of families rather than couples, all parties) must make the effort both to understand the Others and to communicate in such a way that promotes understanding.

The auto maintenance or gourmet cooking are not the only actions that can serve to communicate in a non-verbal language. I was taught early on that "actions speak louder than words" and have never encountered significant evidence to make me believe otherwise. You can speak constantly and loudly of your love for your Other but you cannot out shout your actions. You also cannot out shout your inaction. If all of your protestations of love and caring are verbal and there are no demonstrative acts, it is the apathy of your inaction that will be believed. If your actions appear to have intent that is destructive to the relationship in general or to foundational aspects of the relationship, it will be very difficult indeed to convince your Other that your words are what they should pay attention to. While your actions may be thought of as a language that you create and may well be one that only you and your Other understand, inaction or apathy is pretty much universally recognized. You. Must. Do. Something. If your words are to be believed, you must do something. Remember that your relationship is a dynamic thing. It is always changing. The actions that you took a month ago might have been right and sufficient for the time but now you need to do something else. In terms of the examples already used, automobile maintenance needs to be done periodically. If you just do it once and then let it go, your vehicle will suffer a premature failure. This will also be seen in your relationship. Once you stop working on it, once you cease to do the maintenance that it needs, it will fail. The opposite of love is not hate, it is apathy.

I would not want to have to try listing all of the actions that could substitute for the verbal "I love you too". I do not seek to limit the languages or methods of communication that those in a relationship might use (except to say that I abhor the use of violence in relationships and were it in my power, would not only "limit" it but banish it from the collective psyche). I will however stress that the communication must be ongoing. If you have an action that you use to demonstrate your love and caring and you stop doing that action, the message is clear and unambiguous. There is no reason that you can't change actions. There could well be a situation arise that forces you to change actions. But action there must be. Inaction will be seen as an apathetic lack of communication. If that is not what you intend to be understood, do something.

Desire and Expectation

Do you intrinsically understand the difference between "desire" and "expectation?" Without thinking about it, can you say even to yourself what the difference is? Most folk I ask that question of have the ability to offer a long and rambling or less than clear statement about what the words mean to them. It is crucial to the health of your relationship to have a fully internalized understanding that is compatible with the understanding your spouse has of the concepts. I offer a quick and clear mental picture of the difference.

The Desire

Imagine you have gone out and purchased a lottery ticket for one of the big lotteries. Several tens of millions of dollars are up for grabs. So you buy the ticket and you indulge yourself in a bit of a fantasy about what you would do if you won. You think about the trips you would take, the cars you would drive, former lovers you could flaunt it to (or maybe that's just me), and even the good you could do. You've paid a dollar for your dream, you might as well get your money's worth. You have the "desire" to win the lottery. You have acted on said "desire" by purchasing the ticket. Although the cashier knows about your "desire," no one else needs to. You can keep your fantasy to yourself and if this one does not come through for you, perhaps you will purchase other lottery tickets in the future.

The Expectation

What you don't do is buy the ticket and then immediately walk into your boss' office and tell them just where they can stuff the job. You do not buy the ticket and immediately head to the RV dealership and sign the paperwork on the biggest, most sumptuously appointed motor-home you can find. Even though you have demonstrated a "desire" to win that lottery, you do not have the "expectation" of winning. If you should win that lottery, no one will believe you if you tell them you expected to win. Perhaps it would be more correct to say that you will simply be seen as the lucky one of all those millions of individuals who expected, against all odds, to win the lottery. If you really do expect to win and you want them to believe that, you will need to speak of it convincingly to those you care to tell and quitting your job and buying that RV or yacht, while inadvisable, will demonstrate your expectations (and stupidity).

The Difference

In a relationship, up to and including marriage but certainly not restricted to it, we experience desires and expectations. We want, or desire, any number of behaviors and attitudes from those objects of our affection. Sometimes it just makes sense to communicate those desires. If you want a particular thing for dinner or wish to go to a particular restaurant, you will probably mention it to your significant other. One might wish for a spouse to avoid or engage a specific outfit on specific occasions. Again you might want to mention it, but you also could just play the lottery and hope that your significant other understands what is going on. You may treat your desire like a little fantasy: something that would be great if it happened but that you, for whatever reason, choose to not speak aloud. However, immediately upon moving that desire into the expectation column, you have got to talk.

Your expectations must be made explicit. You must not keep them secret. In the workplace, when starting a new job, one might get a list of responsibilities. Employee handbooks are a common way to disseminate company policy. Other employees may take the initiative to clue a new hire in about just what should or should not be done if the ire of the boss is to be avoided, but this isn't the workplace. It is a dynamic relationship between two or more people (especially if you count children, in-laws, close friends and even work acquaintances) and those do not lend themselves to static solutions or descriptions. Comprehensive marriage manuals do not exist and even if they did, we would probably consider a requirement by a potential spouse to memorize his/her choice of relationship SOP (Standard Operating Procedures) as grounds for backing out of the agreement. You will have to communicate. You will have to inform your mate in no uncertain terms as to what it is you expect of her. You will have to do that every time you expect something of her. If she has not confirmed that she understands what is expected of her, expecting her to do it does nothing but set you up for disappointment.

I am not suggesting that you present a daily or weekly list of demands to your mate. As a matter of fact, for most relationships I would in the strongest terms advise against that very thing. Instead I suggest that you do not expect immediate or continuous telepathy from your mate. Even in those relationships where it really does appear as though they can read each other's minds, there may well come a distracting event. My contention is that unless an expectation has been made clear and agreed upon, you must either take steps to gain

DESIRE & EXPECTATION

that agreement or you must move your "expectation" into the "desire" category. While this can be difficult, it really does not have to be. Say your spouse is a very neat and organized person who straightens up your home daily. You would still need to inform your spouse if you wanted to bring a work mate home for some after office work. It would be wrong for you to assume or expect that the place had been "straightened up" just because it usually is. A long phone call or visit from a distraught friend or relative might be all that is needed to throw off a routine. The phrase "Well it goes without saying that ..." should be banned from the language. It does NOT go without saying. If you did not say it (write it, type it, sign it, draw it, sing it or tap it out in Morse code), there is no justification for believing it is understood. You must communicate your expectations. Not doing so will lead to disappointment and may be the source of trust issues that can be devastating to a relationship.

To not communicate your expectations is to treat your relationship as a lottery. Some people win the lottery but the overwhelming majority of the tickets sold produce nothing more than an unrealized fantasy. Unless that is what you want your relationship to be, you must "explicate" your expectations.

Commonalities and Differences

Generally from one human to the next, there exists huge differences, "for which," to quote my mother on any number of occasions,"praise heaven." The individual you are in a relationship with is just that, an individual. His likes and dislikes, the habits he has acquired, the activities he finds relaxing, the activities he finds stimulating, the information he finds interesting: all of these things and lots more are likely to be different from you as well as different from others you may have been in relationships with.

For a lot of people, even for some Internet or bricks-and-mortar dating services, there is a huge focus on how much you have in common with your potential mate. If you sought the assistance of such a service, you would possibly be evaluated on age, race, build, health, educational background, where you are from, religious beliefs, political beliefs, attitude towards pets (dog person or cat person), and numerous other things, all in the search for that person with whom you are likely to get along. I find this sort of thing to be all well and good but I only expect it to help you find someone you can stand to be around long enough to figure out whether you want to bother investigating the idea of a relationship with them.

Most any divorce lawyer could tell unending stories of folks who appeared to have everything in common, up to and including having kids together (and pets, property, and friends), yet who hate each other's guts, or least find each other annoying to the point of having sought out the lawyer's services in a divorce proceeding. That ought to lead to a little head scratching. If having all those things in common will not save a relationship, why do people want to know and what in the world will save one?

I can make a guess about the first half of that question but as far as the second half goes, I'm on pretty firm ground. They ask you all those things because they are going to metaphorically throw a bunch of stuff at the wall and see what sticks. They have to because that is all they have. As to what will save a relationship or build one that works, that is all in a series of mutual decisions. It is all about active awareness and being honest with yourself. Everything about you or your mate, every tick, habit, trait, belief, physical characteristic, or notion is potential spot for irritation. It is also a potential catalyst for attraction. I have met those who loved a Southern accent and who were attracted to their mate in part because of it. I have also known those who declined to call someone they had met because they had a Southern or Northern accent and they found that irritating. For as much as those things might seem petty, even silly things to allow to strongly affect a relationship, it is good that they were aware enough to see it. Each individual has to decide what about a (potential) significant other is important. Those in the relationship have to decide what is important to the relationship. In every relationship, the important things are the things that those involved decide are important. That is a significant enough truism that it bears stating again. In every relationship, the important things are the things that those involved decide are important.

Philosophically there is a significant difference in what is important to the individual and what is important to the relationship. An Other's height, race or ethnicity, background, intelligence, etc, are not something they can change or compromise on. A decision would simply have to be made as to whether or not those things were important. It is and always has been relative to the situation. If everything else about a potential mate is to your liking but there is this one thing that is exactly like you wish it wasn't, you may choose to decide that one thing is unimportant relative to the overall happiness you experience with that person. That same thing in a relationship where there are several things that aren't exactly as you would wish may be the straw that breaks the camel's back. In both situations it is your decision and no one else is likely to be able to decide for you. Certainly, no dating service will be able to dictate your response to anything.

Most of the things about a potential mate, the tics, habits, traits, beliefs, physical characteristics and notions mentioned above are not digital. They are not on or off, instead they are matters of degree. It is simply too complex to model with a computer or keep up with without one. It is a matter of your personal perception and only you have access to that. Someone else may make a guess, even a really good guess, but in the end, it is still a guess. So it is up to you and to your (potential) mate. You have to look yourself in the mirror and ask yourself, "What is more important, the relationship or this thing that I do not like? Can I be happy with this person the way he is, flaws and all, or can I be happy without this person regardless of his flaws?" The answer to those questions informs your decision.

It should also inform one other thing that I have not yet mentioned. Some of us do things that we believe are cute or popular with our friends without knowing that anyone is irritated by them. Some of the things we do or say we do without conscious thought, we instead do out of habit. Habits can be formed, and habits can be broken. If you communicate with your (potential) mate, it may be that whatever it is that you do not like about her is something that either she is not especially attached to or something that she also does not like about herself. It may well be that she is at least willing to make the effort to change the thing(s) if you mention it. It may be that she values the relationship with you enough to make the effort. So your mirror exercise should inform your decision to communicate with your significant other and inquire if she has any interest in making the effort to change. This has the potential to be a really uncomfortable conversation. For me the earlier on in the relationship it is, the more uncomfortable such a conversation is/would be. Rather obviously, whenever such a communication takes place, diplomacy and clarity should rule the day.

Gender Differences

As a guy, I occasionally find myself arriving back home (if I'm lucky) bleeding, bruised or broken. Usually the physical insults result from my having done something dumb that I either considered fun or thought would be fun when I started it. I am far from being the only guy I know who can make such a claim. The means I have employed to injure myself, while impressively varied, are but a fraction of the ways other guys I either know or know about have used to injure themselves. This is something common with guys. It is something you should be ready to deal with if you are in a relationship with a guy. Of course, I know women as well who undertake ill-advised adventures where injury is a likely outcome but the number of guys who do such things is orders of magnitude greater (in my experience).

Occasionally for whatever reason, I gain access to a bathroom primarily used by one or more females. There are almost always containers in those places that, though clearly labeled, are a complete mystery to me as to the purpose of their contents. I am given to believe that frequently such products pertain to health and beauty maintenance in some manner. Skin care, nail care, hair care, women's plumbing care and more are frequently in residence. I doubt rather seriously that these products are free so I am forced to acknowledge that if I am in a relationship with a female, she will very likely spend money on things the use of which I have no concept. It would probably be a mistake on my part to assume that since I don't know what they do, they aren't really needed and represent a good spot to save some money. I suspect that if I was trying to start a fight, I could just about guarantee one with that tactic. Since I generally consider vehement disagreement something to be avoided in my relationships, it would not be smart of me to verbally dismiss those products as a waste of money. I feel safe in advising other guys to be extremely circumspect in initializing a critical dialogue on anything of a woman's that you do not fully understand.

Men and women are different. For me, that truth is a large part of what makes it worth getting out of bed on any given day. The differences have been celebrated and fought over for all of human history. It is important to note that differences are not automatically incompatibilities. The differences are frequently the very things that attract us to each other. The goal in a relationship like--but not limited to--marriage should not be to recreate the other person in your own image. Rather you should acknowledge the differences and accept them where you must and celebrate them where possible.

Human attraction and interaction is impossibly complex. Anyone who tells you they have it figured out

COMMONALITIES & DIFFERENCES

is most likely lying to you. They might be able to elevate the probability of success but absolutes are simply beyond them. Each individual in a relationship gets to, in fact MUST, decide what about a mate or potential mate is important and what is not. The things you have in common are important only if you decide they are. A common saying is that opposites attract but dating services appear to focus on commonalities, along with the express desires of those employing the service. What will work for you is what you decide will. Your friends and family might pressure you to "like" someone that you don't believe works for you. Remember that no matter how close you are to those friends and family, they will not suffer the pain of any eventual breakup. It is and must be your active decision. You have to be honest with yourself first, closely followed by being honest with your significant other. Telling yourself that you really ought to like someone will not make you like them. Honesty and communication in this are crucial to happiness. If you want to make your relationship work, you must decide that the relationship is what is important and the irritants, differences, and dislikes are something that you can take note of and let go. This is very unlikely to be a static or one time decision. At any point in a relationship, you are likely to be faced with deciding whether you value the relationship more than you are irritated by some quirk your other has acquired. Be the quirk physical, verbal, or something else, you will have to deal with it honestly. If your relationship, like so many, involves a stated vow of commitment, then you both have a duty to each other to come some mutually acceptable agreement. Again, clarity and diplomacy seem like really good ideas to me. Get your point across explicitly but your goal should never be to hurt your other.

Money

As I indicate in this book, there are several things you can do to improve the chances of your relationship being storybook-like in length and intensity. If you take heed of the things that I say, it should be a pretty comfortable existence that you share with your loved one(s). However, there is an eight hundred pound gorilla in the room with the ability to trash all of my good teachings and your honest effort. Money.

Money issues figure into a majority of divorces and probably a significant percentage of breakups that occur prior to the formalization stage. It is one of those things that will be difficult to "work around." You will simply have to meet this one head on and speak frankly and openly to your mate about it (feel free to use this as the opening in that discussion). I would remind you that shouting does not make one's position stronger and neither tears nor apologies will put money back in the bank. The discussion needs to be as rational and devoid of emotion as possible, more of a planning session really. As such, it is probably going to need to happen on a regular basis and fairly frequently at that.

The greater your responsibilities, the greater need you have for savings. If it is just a young you that you are responsible for, you might actually be able to just roll with the punches. You might be able to adjust your life on the fly and throw everything you own in the fully-paid-for station wagon you bought in high school and move some place else and get a different job. As you get a little older and acquire more stuff, that gets a little more difficult. You might want to have enough cash on hand to make emergency trips and to pay the rent and utilities in between jobs. In addition, you might have obligated yourself to things outside of work, community kind of things. Once you are in a relationship, there is usually more stuff. Oddly enough, the two of you will have more than twice as much gear though one would think that you could eliminate a bunch of duplicate kitchen gear and furniture and the like. It just never seems to happen that way. As this is a person you care about, you will want to provide a little more financial cushion against unexpected family emergencies, surprise car repairs and other things that crop up. If in the course of that relationship you purchase a home then you need significant resources available to address plumbing emergencies (yes, you do, even if your home is new), septic repairs, roof damage, cooking disasters, and even just plain old lawn and exterior maintenance. Once you add kids to the mix, you then need extensive savings for all of the things mentioned before plus all of the things that can go wrong or right with a kid. What if your kid shows a knack for music? You will want to encourage that and so you are out the price of a piano and lessons. Sports or smarts: either one could require you to purchase some equipment for the kid to participate and develop. A little sickness or accident might require a long at-home convalescence with either you or your mate staying there with the child, ensuring that you only have one income. Throughout all of this, you will want to have some plan for your retirement in place, not to mention the kid's college fund. An aggressive savings program is certainly indicated.

The funny thing about saving, it is a habit. It is a habit and a skill which must be developed. If you do not have the habit, more money will not cause you to save. Stories abound of lottery winners who have instantly had tens of millions of dollars but were broke or bankrupt just a few years later. If your habit is wasting money, adding more money will just increase the size of the waste pile. If stuff is how you measure your success or wealth, there will never be enough. If you are to develop the habit of saving money, you need to develop the habit early in your financial history, while you typically have very little to worry about. It appears to be easier to increase the amount you set aside than it is to start setting aside some. If one person in a relationship has the saving habit and the other does not, that is a potential spot of friction that can wear right through affection. Ideally, the more fiscally responsible person would have control over the assets but that is not always feasible. Again, you will have to communicate, you will have to have the money conversation and you will need to have it early on in your relationship.

The haste I speak of is necessary because of a particularly insidious and corrosive destroyer of relationships: credit. It does not take long to run up a nearly insurmountable sum on credit. Companies that make their money that way would like nothing more than for you to finance everything through them and have you pay them the lion's share of your "disposable" income for the next 40 years or so. You must avoid this. If the money is not in your pocket, it means you cannot afford a new TV. If you do not have money in the bank sufficient to cover a trip to an unexpected funeral, you cannot afford the new living room suite. Cash is king; it is always the test. Can you pay cash for whatever you want? If not, you cannot afford it. Sometimes it makes good financial sense to have your money in the bank making a higher interest and take out a loan at a lower interest but if you do not have that money in the bank to start with, you cannot afford whatever it is you would like to purchase. Credit WILL kill a relationship, even the strong ones. You have to live somewhere and sometimes, purchasing a home can make sense even if you have to borrow the money. You will need to work within some sensible guidelines though. Think small. The larger the home the more work and more money will be required to keep it up. The larger the home the more furniture you will need to make it look like someone lives there. You want a place that can be heated and cooled very inexpensively. You want a place with no imminent major repairs. Ideally, the cost of the home you purchase should be equal to or less than what you, the couple, can afford on a single salary.

Another dirty little marketing trick to separate you from your hard earned is to use small numbers. Rent-to-own companies typically advertise their prices as a per-week cost. Other companies offer basic services for a very reasonable monthly fee but the add-ons add up very quickly. Cable TV may be the king of that trick. Add just a couple of the things that you just HAVE to have, HBO, Showtime, ESPN 1 thru 50 and an extra room's service and suddenly you are spending serious money. Satellite radio is only a few bucks a month but then so is Internet, so is phone, so are all the other payments. It doesn't take long before you are in over your head. Don't do it. Pay cash and pay up front if possible or if you are especially bad about keeping up (like me). Most of what they are pushing you do not need. Yes, some of it would be nice to have but no, you do not NEED it. You especially do not need it while you cannot afford it.

Financial problems are death to a relationship. The stress such problems induce create issues that will not be constrained. Stress is a major factor in physical disease. Bottling it up inside you will lead to an explosion wherein things will be said that cannot be taken back. Driving with your mind on your money can lead to your spouse collecting a life insurance payout (or having an invalid at home and hundreds of thousands of dollars in medical bills). There is no upside to letting your finances get out of control. The best that you can hope for is that you and your relationship survive but most likely your relationship will not. You need to have the money talk early on and you need to have a plan that you can stick to. Regardless of your intentions, regardless of your love, regardless of your excuses, if your life looks as though you care more about stuff than your relationship, said relationship is in large trouble.

MONEY

All work and no play isn't what is called for either. Your financial plan should include as much recreation as possible. You should do fun stuff together. That fun does not have to be expensive (as a matter of fact, if it is expensive and one of you is responsible, one of you will not be having fun). You have to come up with a plan that works for you but fiscal responsibility has to be a part of it or there will be lots more pain than there is fun.

Pets and Children

Different people attach different levels of importance to different things. The sports car that causes one person to drool might not even be seen by the guy staring at the highly customized motorcycle, even as someone else's pride-and-joy yacht sails by within sight. Plenty of people value experiences rather than stuff so much. They might go on about the concert of a band they had been waiting years to see. A theatrical stage show or movie might spin them up. But for those who have, regardless of the motivation, committed themselves to the responsibility, a pet or a child is likely to be the thing that sits at the top of their value pyramid.

Pets and children are also a potential source of relationship-killing stress. Typically they cause it in different ways but there can be similarities. Pets fall into a couple or more different groups. I think mostly in terms of affectionate and non-affectionate. It is pretty easy to understand how someone gets attached to the dog that is always happy to see you or the cat that curls up in your lap but even if the pet is a snake, fish, or tarantula, what you think about those creatures does not give you reason or permission to simply dismiss your significant other's feelings as unreasonable. You will have to deal respectfully with those feelings and either come to an agreement or reevaluate your commitment to each other. When people describe cats and dogs as members of the family, they aren't kidding. They love their pets. Frequently, they spoil their pets in ways that those who did not raise them from kittens or puppies will never understand and those who study and understand animal training techniques will absolutely deplore.

Imagine looking at a house with an eye towards purchase. You love the house but you hate the neighborhood (or vice versa). Do you say that you will just deal with the thing(s) that you like about the house and ignore the rest of it? Most likely, you do not. We instinctively understand that the house is in the neighborhood and we will have to go through the neighborhood to get to it. Even if we stay at home all the time, we will be in the neighborhood that we hate. You can't really separate one from the other. Relationships work that way too. You can't really honestly say "I love her except ...". You can say that you love her looks. You can say that you love the way he thinks but if you say that you love her or you love him, that statement must be inclusive of everything even if it doesn't describe how you feel about every single aspect of your Significant Other. It is saying that you have evaluated his weird attachment to his pit bulls and decided that you love him anyway. Rather than except you must accept. If you can't do that, if the cats and/or dogs are too much, you should be honest with him and yourself, tell him and move on. The resentment you will engender by effectively banning a beloved pet from a potential mate's life will be difficult if not impossible to overcome. On the other hand, plenty of people are allergic to pet dander. It isn't a willful thing; it is a physiological response over which they have no control. Again, the key is to be honest and open and let your potential mate decide which she values more. Keep in mind that her decision, which may well depend on what stage of the relationship you are in, might not be one complimentary to your ego but you must risk some things if you are to win others.

Children are an exponentially greater stress than pets. If your potential mate has children, then there is a likelihood that there are other adults to consider and interact with as well. It may be the child's other biological parent, the grandparents and/or other extended family members. Any or all of the extended family members with whom you might have to deal could be of the "other" parent, which means they might have no connection to you except through this child that is connected to the person you are interested in. This is not a situation that you should enter into casually or without careful consideration. Even without those other entities, the child may consider you a threat to his relationship with his parent and may undertake actions to try to come between you or simply run you off. There is no guarantee that the person you are interested in will even be able to see what is happening. There is no single approach to handling these situations and were I qualified to tell you specifically what to do, it would require a much more substantial book than this one to address all of the potential pratfalls. My suggestion in this issue, as in all others, is simply to be honest and communicative. Give your potential mate as much reason as possible to trust you and believe what you tell her. Remember though that her first priority is likely to be the child. This is as it should be. A person who does not honor that commitment is unlikely to be the person you are looking for.

Children that don't yet exist can also be problematic. A common and often contentious discussion is that of when in a marriage is the right time to have children. Whether to have children is also a not uncommon point of contention. That they don't (yet) exist does not mean that they don't foster passionate feelings. It is probably not feasible to completely work out all the decisions about such children as you might have or adopt too early in the relationship. It is however, imperative that assumptions not be made, that expectations not be set without benefit of open and honest communication.

Each situation with children or pets must be addressed as its own issue. If you will address them with openness and respect, while avoiding ultimatums and anger, you will get to what should be. It may not be what you would have wished for, but almost no one wants the situation of constant stress that can occur if the issues are addressed badly.

Courtesy

For much of my adult and near adult life I have been perplexed by a phenomenon I have observed several times. Apparently happy couples in a relationship that has already lasted multiple years, to all appearances very much in love and very right for each other, would decide to formalize their relationship and get married. Within six months to a year, they would hate each other's guts and launch into the nastiest of divorces. Had I seen it only once or twice in my years and travels, I would have simply attributed it to chance - sort of the cost of doing business - but it happened frequently enough, and over such a wide spectrum of people of different ages, races, income levels and educational backgrounds, that I figured there must be some causative factor that could be identified and adjusted so as to not be the terribly corrosive force that I had observed.

After much observation and thought, I developed my "Tiptoe Theory." Initially, I thought that living together was simply being married sans ceremony. I was wrong. To this day I do not know or understand why I was wrong, but wrong I was. Getting married changes something in one or both of the participants for many, if not most, couples. In the post honeymoon

COURTESY

era, the couples of the previous paragraph ceased being courteous to each other. They stopped tiptoeing when they knew the other was trying to get some sleep. They allowed the door to slam. No more would they make sure there was fuel in the tank of the car if the Other was to be the next one using the vehicle. In probably a thousand ways, they chose the way that was easiest, or the thing that they liked, without consideration of what effect their spouse might experience. They no longer treated their Significant Other as someone whose continued presence required any effort on their part. They were wrong.

In the minds of most of those I encounter, living together appears to be still thought of as dating, advanced dating to be sure, but still dating. Because of the way living together is perceived, the participants seem to intuitively know that the object of their affection has options, that the loved one can decide that he or she would rather be somewhere else or with someone else and just leave. So, they tiptoe. They are active in their effort to ensure that with them is where their mate wants to be. Many of those who go on to get married believe, for no good reason, that the hard work is done once they kiss the bride/groom. Nothing could be further from the truth. All relationships require effort. All of them require maintenance. If you neglect the relationship completely, all communication is lost and so, there is no relationship. If you neglect it less than completely, the other participants will notice that there are things that you value over your relationship with them. For some relationships that may be okay. I have several friendships where our contact is sporadic and sometimes infrequent. Since that is what we expect, we are okay with that. Marriage though, is not a good choice of relationships for sporadic or infrequent contact. Marriage requires even more tiptoeing. The considerations one provides a spouse need not be physically arduous nor do they necessarily require a lot of mental gymnastics. However, you will have to exert yourself emotionally. You need to not only continue to tiptoe, you need to know that you are doing it out of affection and respect for your mate.

If there is an easy part to being married, it is that in the dating period through experimentation, observation and communication you found out what your mate likes and dislikes (this assumes you were honest with each other during that period as you should have been). Most probably, your spouse will continue to like those things. If she liked it when you opened the door for her, she still will. Favorite foods are still enjoyed. If you will

COURTESY

treat your mate to the things he enjoyed during dating/living together, that will remove much of the threat of a catastrophic meltdown in your relationship. More can be removed if you will simply treat your mate with uncommon courtesy (I wish I could have honestly used the phrase "common courtesy" but I do not see enough of it to believe it to be common). The lack of courtesy informs a mate that you do not care. It is a non-verbal communication but it gets the message across loud and clear that you now take your relationship for granted. Conversely, attentive courtesy lets your mate know that you still value the relationship enough to work for it. Obviously, it cannot be one-sided. One individual cannot do all of the tiptoeing and courtesy necessary to have a happy and successful relationship. It must be reciprocal behavior. Stick with what worked when you were first trying to impress your mate and you will keep what you value.

I have heard it expressed that the opposite of love is not hate, but apathy, not caring at all. I have certainly seen what appeared to be an expression of preference to hatred rather than apathy, if caring or love was unavailable. I think that may be the final clue as to how informally mated couples could go from an apparent loving relationship to the vitriolic speech and behavior of sworn enemies in such a short time. They wanted the other to care and if that caring was not to be expressed as love, they would force it to be as hatred but one way or another, care the other would. The result, however unintended, has to be the saddest of ways for a relationship to end. As painful as the death of a loved one is, the apathy driven death of a relationship is worse, in no small part due to the ease with which it could be avoided. Be courteous to each other and express your caring in whatever manner you choose which cannot be misinterpreted and you will never have to deal with such a reversal of emotional fortune. Continue to tiptoe throughout your time together and keep the relationship fresh.

Continuation of Dating

Marriage is the beginning of a new but not necessarily drastically different phase in a relationship. It represents the evolution of the relationship but it should still contain the elements of what attracted you in the first place.

Dating should not be a con game, a bait and switch, but all too frequently it is. An attractive, courteous, clean and attentive individual is presented as the prize. Then once the ceremony takes place, the weight is gained, the sweats are worn (constantly), things are let go, the door is expected to open itself. If anything were going to scare you away from marriage, this should be it. The only way to know what you are getting is to "make the purchase." To put it bluntly, that sucks.

If you have ever purchased a new car (or a new house or something else), if you are like most of the folks I know, you want to keep it "new" as long as possible. You wash and detail the car frequently. No one is allowed to eat or drink in the vehicle lest they spill something. You want it to look good when you are around friends or family but also when there is no one there but you, you might well stand there and admire it. You learn all of the features it has. You know what happens when you push certain buttons (if you're a guy, you might even read the owner's manual when no one is looking. Women of course, don't feel the need to hide that sort of thing). There is a solid chance that you will follow the recommended maintenance schedule, changing the oil and rotating the tires. Sure, it helps the vehicle keep its value in case you decide to sell it but it brings you pleasure right now to have that beautiful perfect car. Well, it makes no sense at all to value your spouse less than you value your house or car. It makes no sense to take better care of your house or car. Unless you are fairly old or unlucky, you probably will not have your car the rest of your life but if you perform the proper maintenance and care on your relationship, it could well last you until "death do you part." There are certainly those folks who for whatever reason do not care for their new cars or homes. Within months of purchase, their items are prematurely showing their age. Insults build upon insults and in a surprisingly short time, they need (want) a new car. It could well be that their recently pristine chariot no longer functions well, if at all. It is certainly possible to do this to a relationship as well. Relationships need care and they need maintenance. The car you maintain well is generally a safer car. You are less likely to get into an incident with that vehicle.

CONTINUATION OF DATING

You might go so far as to say that the car is taking care of you even as you care for it. The automotive analogy holds up here as well. The relationship with your significant other must also be reciprocal. One partner in the relationship cannot keep it going, you must attend to each other's needs. You must keep each other shiny and new. You must keep yourselves shiny and new for each other.

If you want to keep your relationship fresh, you first need to know and acknowledge what attracted your mate to you in the first place. A little well placed verbal communication should do the trick. You will need to clear your mind of expectations prior to asking. Once you ask your mate "What was it about me that attracted you?" PAY ATTENTION TO THE ANSWER! What actually attracted them to you might not be what you thought. When you make an inquiry of that type, it really isn't the best time to argue (even if you say you are just "discussing"). Listen to your mate and try your best to learn rather than to judge. He is not guaranteed to, or required to, say what you desire him to say. Consider what you found attractive about him. It was probably more than one thing and the initial thing might not be the most important thing in keeping you together. You might have come for the legs beneath that miniskirt and stayed for the brilliant and concise analytical ability. It might have been his skill and coordination on the skateboard that got your attention and his empathy for those less fortunate convinced you to stay. Throw in cooking ability, conversational ability, fun friends, and ten other things. The point is that if you listen, you can find out what is important to your mate and if she will listen, she will find out what is important to you and you can focus on those things and fill in the area around them as life allows you to do.

If on your first few dates, you went to movies and/or out dancing, then (s)he has every right to expect you to be amenable to the idea of going on a date, fairly frequently, after you are married that incorporates those things. She should be able to ask you for such considerations without receiving a rolling of the eyes or an exasperated sigh. He should not be made to feel as though he is somehow asking a terrible inconvenience of you. There are, of course, many potential reasons why something might not be feasible or desirable now even though it was then. But you should always make sure that it is a reason rather than simply an excuse. What is a reason and what is an excuse? Those you will have to work out for yourselves but in general you can think of a reason as why you "can't" and an excuse as why you "won't."

CONTINUATION OF DATING

Over the years I have seen on a number of occasions couples of whom either or both might lounge around the house in sweats or pajamas. Individuals that might forgo a shower for a day or two (or longer) if she is not going out, ignoring the comb and the deodorant and makeup as well. Surely I am not the only one who has seen the woman with huge curlers in her hair and a bathrobe on all weekend long. Then, as soon as the individual plans to go somewhere, the person will have to get cleaned up and perhaps make a trip to the beauty salon or barber shop. He or she breaks out the dressy clothes and begins to remember things like courteous phrases. To me, it looks like the message sent here is that other people, people you don't know, people you know but don't live with, people that you may never see again, are somehow more important than the one to whom you publicly committed. This seems terribly backwards and wrong to me. Why would you not want to look your best for your spouse, for the one you allegedly love above all others? Well, you should. You should get dressed up to stay home from time to time. You should make the place look nice for your spouse rather than waiting for a time when guests are scheduled. Even if life has conspired to make going out too expensive to do as often as you would like, you should clean up and dress up as though you were going out and treat your spouse to an evening with the person that she fell in love with. You should do it often.

In addition to the physical aspects of "date night" (and yes, it is good to have a regular night set as such but, it is bad to believe that on any other night you may be as much of an inconsiderate clown as you like), one should make a regular habit of seducing one's spouse. Flirt with him, have the stereo set to play "your song." Complete (without making a mess of things) one of her normal chores so as to make time for the guiltless seduction. Candles and Barry White on the stereo are the cliche but whatever works for the two of you works for the two of you.

The basic idea is to try to never let a day go by without reminding your mate of why he wanted to be with you. Never take your mate for granted, she has options and life throws curves, sometimes horrible curves. In an ideal world, it is reasonable to want more time with those who are special to you but you have screwed up royally if you ever find yourself regretting that you did not make more of the time that you had. If you are lucky enough to find happiness with another, revel in it and make it last as long as possible.

An Approach to Serious Communication

Verbal communication is a skill that not everyone has. There are as many different approaches to communication as there are reasons to do so. I am not bad at verbal communication, but I am terrible at actually confronting those that I am in a relationship with. A downcast look or, heaven forbid, a tear has been known to make me soften my stance and my statement. At times I have abandoned the effort altogether. Confronting a loved one can be seriously difficult and in any case, will not make verbal communication any easier.

My solution to my wimpiness in that situation is probably not for everyone, but it is something to think about and for those it does work for, you will love it and wonder why you have not been doing it all along. It is a simple solution as far as the instruction in what to do and how to do it but that does not mean the process will be easy or fun. What I do is write a letter. I started this long before either I or anyone else thought of me as a writer. I liked the idea because I was able to take as long as necessary to compose my thoughts and reread them a couple of times so as to make sure that what I said was actually what I meant. I would then call or

AN APPROACH TO SERIOUS COMMUNICATION

visit the individual to whom I was writing and read the letter to her. This part is important. You want the loved one to hear your voice the first time that information is imparted. You want her to know the parts where you were being a little silly or that you meant what you said as humor. You want your other to be able to hear such hurt as there may be in your voice for the sections where that is appropriate. After reading the letter to the other, I would hand the letter to her while expressing the hope that she would reread it and think about the things that I communicated.

Unfortunately, I do not believe that my letter writing has ever salvaged a relationship. Sometimes I think that I waited too long and other times, I think that it was simply that she was "just not that into me." What the letter writing and the reading of it to her did do, was let me know I had done what I could. It let me know that the relationship did not end because she did not understand my willingness or desire to explore further. It let me sleep at night. It also let me move on with certainty. If you put yourself out there like that and can be certain that decisions made are made with full understanding, it makes the ending permanent and allows you to speak to the next potential mate with the confidence that you are totally single and available.

I do not suggest using the letter technique as a reason or method of avoiding confronting your mate. I merely suggest that if confrontation you must have, and trust me, you must, then you should take steps to make it as effective and representative of your thoughts and emotions as possible. You have an ongoing relationship with yourself and respect for yourself is a crucial part of of the success you might have in any other relationship. Whatever you must do to be comfortable with yourself and know that you have dealt with issues squarely will only help you in the long run and make you a more desirable mate to others.

Closing Thoughts

I rather doubt this book will be all things to all people and in truth, it is not intended as such. I want it to be portable, approachable, readable, and useful. I hope I have achieved that but I acknowledge that there are things that may be conspicuous in their absence.

I have not dwelt much on the religious aspects of marriage. As I mention in the introduction, I wanted the concepts mentioned to be useful for relationships other than marriage. I also would point out that there are plenty of religious customs out there that I am not especially familiar with. Even under the aegis of Christianity, the religion I was raised in, I have been to ceremonies that were foreign to me. Still, I contend that if such concepts in this book that do not directly offend one's religion are put into place, it will benefit one's relationship.

I obviously could not directly address every situation that might come up in a marriage or other relationship. If I could, it would still be inadvisable. Most likely it would generate such a massive tome as to violate my desire for it to be approachable (it might still be portable as I expect the digital form of the book to be an option).

CLOSING THOUGHTS

More importantly, I want you to talk. I want you to talk to your Significant Other about the things I mention here but I do not want you to feel like you have to limit the parameters of your discussion to thoughts of mine. I want you to talk to your friends about these concepts. In an ideal world, book clubs will discover this and make it required reading for the next group discussion. I would love for as much of the nation/world as is possible to discuss these concepts and (fingers crossed) embrace them. I am honored if you choose to attribute this to me but I am also honored if relationships improve and marriages last longer even if this book or my name is never mentioned.

A few days after my first meeting with my chosen editors, which happened once most of the writing was done, I did one of the "guy" things I mention in the book and ended up broken. I wrecked a motorcycle and required surgery and care after the fact. My friends and family all were able to avoid continuously telling me what an idiot I was and instead, saw to my needs. Over and above anything I had any reason to expect of them, they saw to my needs. Some of the folks I am thanking in my acknowledgements were not directly influential to this book except that without their assistance, I would have been too caught up in the ancillary aspects

CLOSING THOUGHTS

of day-to-day life, with its attendant sporadic surprises, to actually complete the book. If I can just learn and remember the lessons offered by that situation and apply that learning to my relationships going forward, they can only be more successful.

I sincerely hope I have helped.

APPENDIX 1

My sister that is an editor/advisor for this project, also officiates at weddings and does premarital counseling. One of the things she shared with me is that she has the couples fill out a questionnaire prior to their counseling session(s). She provided me with the sample included below of the type that she uses although the actual questions might change according to certain conditions. The purpose of the questions is to stimulate thought in the couple but, if they are held onto, they can also function as a reminder if things get rough or stale. The questionnaire should be filled out without collaboration between the couple and of course, the information should only be shared, with the express permission of each of the individuals being counseled.

The Counseling Questionnaire

Hey there engaged person!! We need to get going. Please answer the following questions in as much detail as possible, and email your answers to me. We will then set a date for an in-person, premarital counseling session.

1. Explain your understanding of credit.

2. What do you expect from your life as a married person that you do not have in your life as a single person?

3. What do you like best about yourself?

4. For what reasons might sexual intercourse be 'off- limits?'

5. How have you planned and managed your finances as a single person?

6. Please list NO LESS than five (5) reasons that you want to get married.

7. What are the reasons you want to marry _____? Please list NO LESS than five (5) reasons.

8. How do you create and increase intimacy with _____?

9. What do you like least about yourself?

10. What role does faith/religion/spirituality plan in your daily life?

11. Do you plan on having children? If so, why?

The following is a sample of the ceremony as I am likely to perform it. Rather obviously, the readings can be selected by the couple either from options I provide or something they've found that speaks to them. The exact verbiage of the vows and the exchanging of rings is also likely to change from one ceremony to the next. Of course, the couple gets to (must) approve the final draft of the ceremony. Generally I like to have the ceremony printed out on heavy paper which I place in a nice folder. After the ceremony, usually at the reception, I present the print version of the ceremony to the couple as a keepsake, sometimes as a part of a toast. The gesture has been very well received so far.

month day, yearAD

A SPECIAL CELEBRATION

THE PUBLIC WEDDING VOWS OF
MR. His Name
&
MS Her Name

REV S.M. DUPREE OFFICIATING

Wedding Ceremony

PROCESSIONAL

w/music

OPENING WORDS OF THE OFFICIANT

Dearly Beloved, we gather here today, in the presence of these witnesses, to celebrate and acknowledge the commitment Her Name and His Name have already made to each other. They have been completely and totally together for long enough now that for many of us, this day appeared inevitable. Even as they've struggled with challenges and changes that neither could have imagined, they've learned to live, love and work TOGETHER. Today, we witness the marriage of Love and Art (or Respect and Dedication or some other two vital elements). Today, they will profess verbally that which has been in their hearts and minds for some time…

WITNESS ACKNOWLEDGEMENT

Allow me to congratulate you all on being invited to attend this special event. Your presence here today means that very likely, you will be witnesses not just to this wedding ceremony but, to the marriage as well. As such, I charge you to accept your responsibility to always act and speak in a way that acknowledges and respects the love that His Name and Her Name have and have professed for each other. Your words and acts can and will affect this couple's relationship. Let all of those words and actions be chosen out of love. Will you do this? If so, answer "I will".

AN OPENING READING

A poem by Charles Morris

Are we to love Beauty
Or, are we to love Possession?

Possession is a clutch of ravage
that searches for an idol

Beauty is a priceless carriage
that markets for the bridle

Beauty is a treasured flower
that cloaks eternal with the Spring

And Possession with all its hours
could never clothe the dream

DEFINITION OF MARRIAGE

Steve: Marriage represents our efforts to remove doubt from our committed relationships. It frees us from the fears and insecurities that fuel so many stories of teen-aged and early adult angst. When one is in a truly mutually committed relationship, one if finally free to love as one deems appropriate. It represents the enthusiastic acceptance of the expanded responsibilities that the relationship will bring. It allows us to focus our energies and attention on our chosen mate without need to explain or justify. If you are approaching it with the proper attitude, it is a very desirable expansion of personal freedom(s).

VOWS

Her Name do you take His Name to be your lawfully wedded husband? To love, respect and care for him through times of DOUBT and times of CONFIDENCE, through times of WEAKNESS and times of VIGOR, times of WANT and times of ABUNDANCE, times of SORROW and times of JOY?

Her Name: I do.

His Name do you take Her Name to be your lawfully wedded wife? To love, respect and care for her through times of DOUBT and times of CONFIDENCE, through times of WEAKNESS and times of VIGOR, times of WANT and times of ABUNDANCE, times of SORROW and times of JOY?

His Name: I do.

EXCHANGE OF RINGS

Steve: Please repeat after me:
Him, I give you this ring as a symbol of our love and my commitment to you. With it I wed you and give you my body, soul and heart.
Her, I give you this ring as a symbol of our love and my commitment to you. With it I wed you and give you my body, soul and heart.

SECOND READING

"Wedding Blessing"
~ Author Unknown ~

Treat yourselves and each other with respect, and remind yourselves often of what brought you together. Give the highest priority to the tenderness, gentleness and kindness that your connection deserves. When frustration, difficulties and fear assail your relationship- as they threaten all relationships at one time or another-- remember to focus on what is right between you, not only the part which seems wrong. In this way, you can ride out the storm clouds that may hide the face of the sun in your lives- remembering that even if you lost sight of it for a moment, the sun is still there. And if each of you takes responsibility for the quality of life together, it will be marked by abundance and delight.

THE PRONOUNCEMENT

Him and Her

You have exchanged your vows and made your promises with eyes wide open and hearts filled with love. You have given and received the rings which will symbolize this solemn union.
With the blessing and support of your family and friends,
I now pronounce you...
HUSBAND and WIFE.

You may now kiss the groom!
Ladies and Gentlemen, I am happy and proud to present Them.

INVITATION TO CELEBRATION

All are invited to celebrate with and congratulate the happy couple at the reception.
Please respect the venue, each other and, please have fun.

The Author

In high school only one guy was in ROTC, choir, Audio-Visual club, and Drama club: Stephen M. Dupree. That broad spectrum of interests continues to this day and has even expanded. Raising large breed dogs, brewing and consuming craft beers, bicycling, motorcycling, politics, science fiction, travel, and of course, writing, have been added to the list of things in which he dabbles. That list is not nearly comprehensive but serves to demonstrate the breadth of his curiosity. The diversity of his avocations may be explained by his long term passion for observing and analyzing human interaction, specifically, the nature of relationships and what we get wrong, right and otherwise.

A native and current resident of Knoxville, TN and citizen of the world, Dupree has a stated willingness to be where the Universe sends him. There are many more things he would happily consent to discuss over a pint of a good brewer's finest.

www.ingramcontent.com/pod-product-compliance
Lightning Source LLC
LaVergne TN
LVHW021411080426
835508LV00020B/2558